The Bible on

FAITH, LOVE,

AND HOPE

The Bible on
FAITH, LOVE, AND HOPE

GRAMERCY BOOKS
• NEW YORK •

This 1997 edition is published by Gramercy Books,
a division of Random House Value Publishing, Inc.
201 East 50th Street, New York, New York 10022.

Gramercy Books and colophon are trademarks of
Random House Value Publishing, Inc.

Random House
New York • Toronto • London • Sydney • Auckland
http://www.randomhouse.com/

Printed and bound in the United States of America

COMPILED, EDITED, DESIGNED, AND COMPOSITED BY FRANK J. FINAMORE

A CIP catalog record for this book is available from the Library of Congress.

The Bible on Faith, Love, and Hope
ISBN 0–517–18387–0

8 7 6 5 4 3 2 1

CONTENTS

INTRODUCTION

The Bible is without a doubt one of the greatest books ever written. If you are a believer it is a work of divine inspiration, which would easily account for its greatness. But one does not have to be religious to be astonished or inspired by the words of the Bible, as this collection proves. Gathered in this volume are some of the most famous and beautiful passages from the Old and New Testaments, from the book of Genesis to the book of Revelation.

There is something inexplicably awe-inspiring about the language of the King James Bible, from which the selections in this book have been taken. The quality of the language is of Shakespearean power and beauty. The words resonate with a poetic majesty and emotion befitting the subject matter. The King James Bible captures the grandeur and scope of the original Greek and Hebrew in a way no other English translation ever has or ever will. Whether proclaiming the heartfelt faith of the famous Psalm 23 ("The Lord is my sheperd: I shall not want") or revealing the words of Christ in the Gospels, there is the unmistakable stamp of true revelation.

But *The Bible on Faith, Love, and Hope* is not just for the faithful. Gathered in this volume are the timeless words and thoughts of mankind's greatest prophets, heroes, and heroines. Ones does not have to be religious to be moved by these words. The Bible is the emotional and personal record of mankind's evolving relationship with God, a repository of man's greatest hopes and beliefs from times of desperation and despair to times of victory and exultation.

Reading these inspired words, one will rediscover the promise of faith, the fulfillment of hope, and the prophecy of love contained in the eternal mystery that is God. For hundreds of years they have comforted people in times of difficulty and disaster. The power of the words of the Bible defies explanation. Whether they are of holy provenance or not, is a matter of personal belief. One can only say they represent some of the most divine thoughts and aspirations of humanity.

FRANK JAMES FINAMORE

New York, 1997

FAITH

They provoked him to jealousy with strange gods, with abominations provoked they him to anger.

They sacrificed unto devils, not to God; to gods whom they knew not, to new gods that came newly up, whom your fathers feared not.

Of the Rock that begat thee thou art unmindful, and hast forgotten God that formed thee.

And when the Lord saw it, he abhorred them, because of the provoking of his sons, and of his daughters.

And he said, I will hide my face from them, I will see what their end shall be: for they are a very froward generation, children in whom is no faith.

DEUTERONOMY 32:16-20

Then said David to the Philistine, Thou comest to me with a sword, and with a spear, and with a shield: but I come to thee in the name of the Lord of hosts, the God of the armies of Israel, whom thou hast defied.

This day will the Lord deliver thee into mine hand; and I will smite thee, and take thine head from thee; and I will give the carcases of the host of the Philistines this day unto the fowls of the air, and to the wild beasts of the earth; that all the earth may know that there is a God in Israel.

1 SAMUEL 17:45-46

And he said, Hearken ye, all Judah, and ye inhabitants of Jerusalem, and thou king Jehoshaphat, thus saith the Lord unto you, Be not afraid nor dismayed by reason of this great multitude; for the battle is not yours, but God's.

Tomorrow go ye down against them: behold, they come up by the cliff of Ziz; and ye shall find them at the end of the brook, before the wilderness of Jeruel.

Ye shall not need to fight in this battle: set yourselves, stand ye still, and see the salvation of the Lord with you, O Judah and Jerusalem: fear not, nor be dismayed; tomorrow go out against them: for the Lord will be with you.

And Jehoshaphat bowed his head with his face to the ground: and all Judah and the inhabitants of Jerusalem fell before the Lord, worshipping the Lord.

And the Levites, of the children of the Kohathites, and of the children of the Korhites, stood up to praise the Lord God of Israel with a loud voice on high.

And they rose early in the morning, and went forth into the wilderness of Tekoa: and as they went forth, Jehoshaphat stood and said, Hear me, O Judah, and ye inhabitants of Jerusalem. Believe in the Lord your God, so shall ye be established; believe his prophets, so shall ye prosper.

And when he had consulted with the people, he appointed singers unto the Lord, and that should praise the beauty of holiness, as they went out before the army, and to say, Praise the Lord; for his mercy endureth forever.

2 CHRONICLES 20:15-21

I will love thee, O Lord, my strength.
The Lord is my rock, and my fortress, and my deliverer; my God, my strength, in whom I will trust; my buckler, and the horn of my salvation, and my high tower.

I will call upon the Lord, who is worthy to be praised: so shall I be saved from mine enemies.

The sorrows of death compassed me, and the floods of ungodly men made me afraid.

The sorrows of hell compassed me about: the snares of death prevented me.

In my distress I called upon the Lord, and cried unto my God: he heard my voice out of his temple, and my cry came before him, even into his ears.

Then the earth shook and trembled; the foundations also of the hills moved and were shaken, because he was wroth.

There went up a smoke out of his nostrils, and fire out of his mouth devoured: coals were kindled by it.

He bowed the heavens also, and came down: and darkness was under his feet.

And he rode upon a cherub, and did fly: yea, he did fly upon the wings of the wind.

He made darkness his secret place; his pavilion round about him were dark waters and thick clouds of the skies.

At the brightness that was before him his thick clouds passed, hail stones and coals of fire.

The Lord also thundered in the heavens, and the Highest gave his voice; hail stones and coals of fire.

Yea, he sent out his arrows, and scattered them; and he shot out lightnings, and discomfited them.

Then the channels of waters were seen, and the foundations of the world were discovered at thy rebuke, O Lord, at the blast of the breath of thy nostrils.

He sent from above, he took me, he drew me out of many waters.

He delivered me from my strong enemy, and from them which hated me: for they were too strong for me.

They prevented me in the day of my calamity: but the Lord was my stay.

He brought me forth also into a large place; he delivered me, because he delighted in me.

The Lord rewarded me according to my righteousness; according to the cleanness of my hands hath he recompensed me.

For I have kept the ways of the Lord, and have not wickedly departed from my God.

For all his judgments were before me, and I did not put away his statutes from me.

I was also upright before him, and I kept myself from mine iniquity.

Therefore hath the Lord recompensed me according to my righteousness, according to the cleanness of my hands in his eyesight.

With the merciful thou wilt show thyself merciful; with an upright man thou wilt show thyself upright;

With the pure thou wilt show thyself pure; and with the froward thou wilt show thyself froward.

For thou wilt save the afflicted people; but wilt bring down high looks.

For thou wilt light my candle: the Lord my God will enlighten my darkness.

For by thee I have run through a troop; and by my God have I leaped over a wall.

As for God, his way is perfect: the word of the Lord is tried: he is a buckler to all those that trust in him.

For who is God save the Lord? or who is a rock save
our God?

It is God that girdeth me with strength, and maketh
my way perfect.

He maketh my feet like hinds' feet, and setteth me
upon my high places.

He teacheth my hands to war, so that a bow of steel is
broken by mine arms.

Thou hast also given me the shield of thy salvation:
and thy right hand hath holden me up, and thy
gentleness hath made me great.

Thou hast enlarged my steps under me, that my feet
did not slip.

I have pursued mine enemies, and overtaken them:
neither did I turn again till they were consumed.

I have wounded them that they were not able to rise:
they are fallen under my feet.

For thou hast girded me with strength unto the battle:
thou hast subdued under me those that rose up
against me.

Thou hast also given me the necks of mine enemies;
that I might destroy them that hate me.

They cried, but there was none to save them: even
unto the Lord, but he answered them not.

Then did I beat them small as the dust before the
wind: I did cast them out as the dirt in the streets.

Thou hast delivered me from the strivings of the people; and thou hast made me the head of the heathen: a people whom I have not known shall
serve me.

As soon as they hear of me, they shall obey me: the
strangers shall submit themselves unto me.

The strangers shall fade away, and be afraid out of
their close places.

The Lord liveth; and blessed be my rock; and let the
God of my salvation be exalted.

It is God that avengeth me, and subdueth the people
under me.
He delivereth me from mine enemies: yea, thou liftest
me up above those that rise up against me: thou
hast delivered me from the violent man.
Therefore will I give thanks unto thee, O Lord, among
the heathen, and sing praises unto thy name.
Great deliverance giveth he to his king; and showeth
mercy to his anointed, to David, and to his seed
forevermore.

PSALM 18

The Lord is my shepherd; I shall not want.
He maketh me to lie down in green pastures:
he leadeth me beside the still waters.
He restoreth my soul: he leadeth me in the paths of
righteousness for his name's sake.
Yea, though I walk through the valley of the shadow
of death, I will fear no evil: for thou art with me;
thy rod and thy staff they comfort me.
Thou preparest a table before me in the presence of
mine enemies: thou anointest my head with oil;
my cup runneth over.
Surely goodness and mercy shall follow me all the
days of my life: and I will dwell in the house of
the Lord forever.

PSALM 23

The Lord is my light and my salvation; whom shall I fear? the Lord is the strength of my life; of whom shall I be afraid?

PSALM 27:1

My soul, wait thou only upon God; for my expectation is from him.
He only is my rock and my salvation: he is my defense; I shall not be moved.
In God is my salvation and my glory: the rock of my strength, and my refuge, is in God.
Trust in him at all times; ye people, pour out your heart before him: God is a refuge for us. Selah.

PSALM 62:5-8

He that dwelleth in the secret place of the most High shall abide under the shadow of the Almighty.
I will say of the Lord, He is my refuge and my fortress: my God; in him will I trust.
Surely he shall deliver thee from the snare of the fowler, and from the noisome pestilence.
He shall cover thee with his feathers, and under his wings shalt thou trust: his truth shall be thy shield and buckler.
Thou shalt not be afraid for the terror by night; nor for the arrow that flieth by day;
Nor for the pestilence that walketh in darkness; nor for the destruction that wasteth at noonday.

A thousand shall fall at thy side, and ten thousand at
  thy right hand; but it shall not come nigh thee.
Only with thine eyes shalt thou behold and see the
  reward of the wicked.
Because thou hast made the Lord, which is my refuge,
  even the most High, thy habitation;
There shall no evil befall thee, neither shall any
  plague come nigh thy dwelling.
For he shall give his angels charge over thee, to keep
  thee in all thy ways.
They shall bear thee up in their hands, lest thou dash
  thy foot against a stone.
Thou shalt tread upon the lion and adder: the young
  lion and the dragon shalt thou trample under feet.
Because he hath set his love upon me, therefore will I
  deliver him: I will set him on high, because he
  hath known my name.
He shall call upon me, and I will answer him: I will
  be with him in trouble; I will deliver him, and
  honour him.
With long life will I satisfy him, and show him my
  salvation.

PSALM 91:1-16

The Lord is on my side; I will not fear: what can
man do unto me?
The Lord taketh my part with them that help
me: therefore shall I see my desire upon them that
hate me.
It is better to trust in the Lord than to put confidence
in man.

PSALM 118:6-8

A talebearer revealeth secrets: but he that is of a faithful spirit concealeth the matter.

PROVERBS 11:13

M ost men will proclaim everyone his own goodness: but a faithful man who can find?
The just man walketh in his integrity: his children are blessed after him.

PROVERBS 20:6-7

F aithful are the wounds of a friend; but the kisses of an enemy are deceitful.

PROVERBS 27:6

A faithful man shall abound with blessings: but he that maketh haste to be rich shall not be innocent.

PROVERBS 28:20

In that day shall this song be sung in the land of Judah: We have a strong city; salvation will God appoint for walls and bulwarks.

Open ye the gates, that the righteous nation which keepeth the truth may enter in.

Thou wilt keep him in perfect peace, whose mind is stayed on thee: because he trusteth in thee.

Trust ye in the Lord forever: for in the Lord Jehovah is everlasting strength.

ISAIAH 26:1-4

I am the Lord, and there is none else, there is no God beside me: I girded thee, though thou hast not known me:

That they may know from the rising of the sun, and from the west, that there is none beside me. I am the Lord, and there is none else.

I form the light, and create darkness: I make peace, and create evil: I the Lord do all these things.

Drop down, ye heavens, from above, and let the skies pour down righteousness: let the earth open, and let them bring forth salvation, and let righteousness spring up together; I the Lord have created it.

ISAIAH 45:5-8

Lift up your eyes to the heavens, and look upon the earth beneath: for the heavens shall vanish away like smoke, and the earth shall wax old like a garment, and they that dwell therein shall die in like manner: but my salvation shall be forever, and my righteousness shall not be abolished.

ISAIAH 51:6

Shadrach, Meshach, and Abednego answered and said to the king, O Nebuchadnezzar, we are not careful to answer thee in this matter.

If it be so, our God whom we serve is able to deliver us from the burning fiery furnace, and he will deliver us out of thine hand, O king.

But if not, be it known unto thee, O king, that we will not serve thy gods, nor worship the golden image which thou hast set up.

Then was Nebuchadnezzar full of fury, and the form of his visage was changed against Shadrach, Meshach, and Abednego: therefore he spake, and commanded that they should heat the furnace seven times more than it was wont to be heated.

And he commanded the most mighty men that were in his army to bind Shadrach, Meshach, and Abednego, and to cast them into the burning fiery furnace.

Then these men were bound in their coats, their stockings, and their hats, and their other garments, and were cast into the midst of the burning fiery furnace.

Therefore because the king's commandment was urgent, and the furnace exceeding hot, the flame of the fire slew those men that took up Shadrach, Meshach, and Abednego.

And these three men, Shadrach, Meshach, and Abednego fell down bound into the midst of the burning fiery furnace.

Then Nebuchadnezzar the king was astounded, and rose up in haste, and spake, and said unto his counsellors, Did not we cast three men bound into the midst of the fire? They answered and said unto the king, True, O king.

He answered and said, Lo, I see four men loose, walking in the midst of the fire, and they have no hurt; and the form of the fourth is like the Son of God.

Then Nebuchadnezzar came near to the mouth of the burning fiery furnace, and spake, and said, Shadrach, Meshach, and Abednego, ye servants of the most high God, come forth, and come hither. Then Shadrach, Meshach, and Abednego, came forth of the midst of the fire.

DANIEL 3:16-26

I will stand upon my watch, and set me upon the tower, and will watch to see what he will say unto me, and what I shall answer when I am reproved.

And the Lord answered me, and said, Write the vision, and make it plain upon tables, that he may run that readeth it.

For the vision is yet for an appointed time, but at the end it shall speak, and not lie: though it tarry, wait for it; because it will surely come, it will not tarry. Behold, his soul which is lifted up is not upright in him: but the just shall live by his faith.

HABAKKUK 2:1-4

Wherefore, if God so clothe the grass of the field, which today is, and tomorrow is cast into the oven, shall he not much more clothe you, O ye of little faith?

Therefore take no thought, saying, What shall we eat? or, What shall we drink? or, Wherewithal shall we be clothed?

(For after all these things do the Gentiles seek:) for your heavenly Father knoweth that ye have need of all these things.

But seek ye first the kingdom of God, and his righteousness; and all these things shall be added unto you.

Take therefore no thought for the morrow: for the morrow shall take thought for the things of itself. Sufficient unto the day is the evil thereof.

MATTHEW 6:30-34

And when Jesus was entered into Capernaum, there came unto him a centurion, beseeching him,

And saying, Lord, my servant lieth at home sick of the palsy, grievously tormented.

And Jesus saith unto him, I will come and heal him.

The centurion answered and said, Lord, I am not worthy that thou shouldest come under my roof: but speak the word only, and my servant shall be healed.

For I am a man under authority, having soldiers under me: and I say to this man, Go, and he goeth; and to another, Come, and he cometh; and to my servant, Do this, and he doeth it.

When Jesus heard it, he marvelled, and said to them that followed, Verily I say unto you, I have not found so great faith, no, not in Israel.

And I say unto you, That many shall come from the east and west, and shall sit down with Abraham, and Isaac, and Jacob, in the kingdom of heaven.

But the children of the kingdom shall be cast out into outer darkness: there shall be weeping and gnashing of teeth.

And Jesus said unto the centurion, Go thy way; and as thou hast believed, so be it done unto thee. And his servant was healed in the selfsame hour.

MATTHEW 8:5-13

And, behold, there arose a great tempest in the sea, insomuch that the ship was covered with the waves: but he was asleep.

And his disciples came to him, and awoke him, saying, Lord, save us: we perish.

And he saith unto them, Why are ye fearful, O ye of little faith? Then he arose, and rebuked the winds and the sea; and there was a great calm.

MATTHEW 8:24-26

And, behold, they brought to him a man sick of the palsy, lying on a bed: and Jesus seeing their faith said unto the sick of the palsy, Son, be of good cheer; thy sins be forgiven thee.

MATTHEW 9:2

And Jesus arose, and followed him, and so did his disciples.

And, behold, a woman, which was diseased with an issue of blood twelve years, came behind him, and touched the hem of his garment;

For she said within herself, If I may but touch his garment, I shall be whole.

But Jesus turned him about, and when he saw her, he said, Daughter, be of good comfort; thy faith hath made thee whole. And the woman was made whole from that hour.

MATTHEW 9:19-22

And when he was come into the house, the blind men came to him: and Jesus saith unto them, Believe ye that I am able to do this? They said unto him, Yea, Lord.

Then touched he their eyes, saying, According to your faith be it unto you.

MATTHEW 9:29

He saith unto them, But whom say ye that I am?

And Simon Peter answered and said, Thou art the Christ, the Son of the living God.

And Jesus answered and said unto him, Blessed art thou, Simon Barjona: for flesh and blood hath not revealed it unto thee, but my Father which is in heaven.

And I say also unto thee, That thou art Peter, and upon this rock I will build my church; and the gates of hell shall not prevail against it.

And I will give unto thee the keys of the kingdom of heaven: and whatsoever thou shalt bind on earth shall be bound in heaven: and whatsoever thou shalt loose on earth shall be loosed in heaven.

MATTHEW 16:15-19

And when they were come to the multitude, there came to him a certain man, kneeling down to him, and saying,

Lord, have mercy on my son: for he is a lunatic, and sore vexed: for ofttimes he falleth into the fire, and oft into the water.

And I brought him to thy disciples, and they could not cure him.

Then Jesus answered and said, O faithless and perverse generation, how long shall I be with you? how long shall I suffer you? bring him hither to me.

And Jesus rebuked the devil; and he departed out of him: and the child was cured from that very hour.

Then came the disciples to Jesus apart, and said, Why could not we cast him out?

And Jesus said unto them, Because of your unbelief: for verily I say unto you, If ye have faith as a grain of mustard seed, ye shall say unto this mountain, Remove hence to yonder place; and it shall remove; and nothing shall be impossible unto you.

MATTHEW 17:14-20

For whosoever will save his life shall lose it; but whosoever shall lose his life for my sake and the gospel's, the same shall save it.

For what shall it profit a man, if he shall gain the whole world, and lose his own soul?

MARK 8:35-36

Jesus said unto him, If thou canst believe, all things are possible to him that believeth.

MARK 9:23

And Jesus answering saith unto them, Have faith in God.

For verily I say unto you, That whosoever shall say unto this mountain, Be thou removed, and be thou cast into the sea; and shall not doubt

in his heart, but shall believe that those things
which he saith shall come to pass; he shall have
whatsoever he saith.

Therefore I say unto you, Whatever things ye desire,
when ye pray, believe that ye receive them, and ye
shall have them.

And when ye stand praying, forgive, if ye have ought
against any: that your Father also which is in
heaven may forgive you your trespasses.

But if ye do not forgive, neither will your Father which
is in heaven forgive your trespasses.

Mark 11:22-26

A nd he said unto them, Go ye into all the
world, and preach the gospel to every creature.
He that believeth and is baptized shall be saved;
but he that believeth not shall be damned.

And these signs shall follow them that believe: In my
name shall they cast out devils; they shall speak
with new tongues;

They shall take up serpents; and if they drink any
deadly thing, it shall not hurt them; they shall lay
hands on the sick, and they shall recover.

Mark 16:15-18

ut as many as received him, to them gave he
power to become the sons of God, even to
them that believe on his name;
Which were born, not of blood, nor of the will of
the flesh, nor of the will of man, but of God.
And the Word was made flesh, and dwelt among us
(and we beheld his glory, the glory as of the only
begotten of the Father), full of grace and truth.

JOHN 1:12-14

f I have told you earthly things, and ye believe
not, how shall ye believe, if I tell you of heavenly things?
And no man hath ascended up to heaven, but he
that came down from heaven, even the Son of
man which is in heaven.
And as Moses lifted up the serpent in the wilderness,
even so must the Son of man be lifted up:
That whosoever believeth in him should not perish,
but have eternal life.
For God so loved the world, that he gave his only
begotten Son, that whosoever believeth in him
should not perish, but have everlasting life.
For God sent not his Son into the world to condemn
the world; but that the world through him might
be saved.
He that believeth on him is not condemned: but he
that believeth not is condemned already, because
he hath not believed in the name of the only
begotten Son of God.

JOHN 3:12-18

For had ye believed Moses, ye would have believed me: for he wrote of me.

JOHN 5:46

For I came down from heaven, not to do mine own will, but the will of him that sent me. And this is the Father's will which hath sent me, that of all which he hath given me I should lose nothing, but should raise it up again at the last day.
And this is the will of him that sent me, that everyone which seeth the Son, and believeth on him, may have everlasting life: and I will raise him up at the last day.

JOHN 6:38-40

I am the door: by me if any man enter in, he shall be saved, and shall go in and out, and find pasture.

JOHN 10:9

Then Martha, as soon as she heard that Jesus was coming, went and met him: but Mary sat still in the house.
Then said Martha unto Jesus, Lord, if thou hadst been here, my brother had not died.

But I know, that even now, whatsoever thou wilt ask
of God, God will give it thee.

Jesus saith unto her, Thy brother shall rise again.

Martha saith unto him, I know that he shall rise again
in the resurrection at the last day.

Jesus said unto her, I am the resurrection, and the life:
he that believeth in me, though he were dead, yet
shall he live.

And whosoever liveth and believeth in me shall
never die. Believest thou this?

She saith unto him, Yea, Lord: I believe that thou art
the Christ, the Son of God, which should come
into the world.

And when she had so said, she went her way, and
called Mary her sister secretly, saying, The Master
is come, and calleth for thee.

As soon as she heard that, she arose quickly, and came
unto him.

Now Jesus was not yet come into the town, but was
in that place where Martha met him.

JOHN 11:20-30

Then Jesus said unto them, Yet a little while is
the light with you. Walk while ye have the
light, lest darkness come upon you: for he that
walketh in darkness knoweth not whither he
goeth.

While ye have light, believe in the light, that ye may
be the children of light. These things spake Jesus,
and departed, and did hide himself from them.

JOHN 12:35-36

Let not your heart be troubled: ye believe in God, believe also in me.

JOHN 14:1

Believe me that I am in the Father, and the Father in me: or else believe me for the very works' sake.

JOHN 14:11

Jesus saith unto him, Thomas, because thou hast seen me, thou hast believed: blessed are they that have not seen, and yet have believed.

And many other signs truly did Jesus in the presence of his disciples, which are not written in this book;

But these are written, that ye might believe that Jesus is the Christ, the Son of God; and that believing ye might have life through his name.

JOHN 20:29-31

Where is boasting then? It is excluded. By what law? of works? Nay: but by the law of faith.

Therefore we conclude that a man is justified by faith without the deeds of the law.

Is he the God of the Jews only? Is he not also of the
Gentiles? Yes, of the Gentiles also,
Seeing it is one God, which shall justify the circumci-
sion by faith, and uncircumcision through faith.
Do we then make void the law through faith? God for-
bid: yea, we establish the law.

ROMANS 3:27-31

Therefore it is of faith, that it might be by grace;
to the end the promise might be sure to all the
seed; not to that only which is of the law, but
to that also which is of the faith of Abraham; who
is the father of us all,
(As it is written, I have made thee a father of many
nations), before him whom he believed, even God,
who quickeneth the dead, and calleth those things
which be not as though they were.
Who against hope believed in hope, that he might
become the father of many nations, according to
that which was spoken, So shall thy seed be.
And being not weak in faith, he considered not his
own body now dead, when he was about a hundred years old, neither yet the deadness of Sarah's
womb:
He staggered not at the promise of God through unbelief; but was strong in faith, giving glory to God;
And being fully persuaded that, what he had
promised, he was able also to perform.

ROMANS 4:16-21

For we walk by faith, not by sight.

2 CORINTHIANS 5:7

Knowing that a man is not justified by the works of the law, but by the faith of Jesus Christ, even we have believed in Jesus Christ, that we might be justified by the faith of Christ, and not by the works of the law: for by the works of the law shall no flesh be justified.

GALATIANS 2:16

I am crucified with Christ: nevertheless I live; yet not I, but Christ liveth in me: and the life which I now live in the flesh I live by the faith of the Son of God, who loved me, and gave himself for me.

GALATIANS 2:20

Know ye therefore that they which are of faith, the same are the children of Abraham. And the scripture, foreseeing that God would justify the heathen through faith, preached before the gospel unto Abraham, saying, In thee shall all nations be blessed.

So then they which be of faith are blessed with faithful Abraham.

For as many as are of the works of the law are under the curse: for it is written, Cursed is everyone that continueth not in all things which are written in the book of the law to do them.

But that no man is justified by the law in the sight of God, it is evident: for, The just shall live by faith.

And the law is not of faith: but, The man that doeth them shall live in them.

Christ hath redeemed us from the curse of the law, being made a curse for us: for it is written, Cursed is everyone that hangeth on a tree;

That the blessing of Abraham might come on the Gentiles through Jesus Christ; that we might receive the promise of the Spirit through faith.

GALATIANS 3:7-14

Christ is become of no effect unto you, whosoever of you are justified by the law; ye are fallen from grace.

For we through the Spirit wait for the hope of righteousness by faith.

For in Jesus Christ neither circumcision availeth anything, nor uncircumcision; but faith which worketh by love.

GALATIANS 5:4-6

There is one body, and one Spirit, even as ye are called in one hope of your calling; One Lord, one faith, one baptism, One God and Father of all, who is above all, and through all, and in you all. But unto every one of us is given grace according to the measure of the gift of Christ.

EPHESIANS 4:4-7

Wherefore take unto you the whole armour of God, that ye may be able to withstand in the evil day, and having done all, to stand. Stand therefore, having your loins girt about with truth, and having on the breastplate of righteousness; And your feet shod with the preparation of the gospel of peace; Above all, taking the shield of faith, wherewith ye shall be able to quench all the fiery darts of the wicked.

EPHESIANS 6:13-16

This is a faithful saying, and worthy of all acceptation, that Christ Jesus came into the world to save sinners; of whom I am chief.

1 TIMOTHY 1:15

ight the good fight of faith, lay hold on eternal life, whereunto thou art also called, and hast professed a good profession before many witnesses.

1 TIMOTHY 6:12

ow faith is the substance of things hoped for, the evidence of things not seen.
For by it the elders obtained a good report.
Through faith we understand that the worlds were framed by the word of God, so that things which are seen were not made of things which do appear.
By faith Abel offered unto God a more excellent sacrifice than Cain, by which he obtained witness that he was righteous, God testifying of his gifts: and by it he being dead yet speaketh.
By faith Enoch was translated that he should not see death; and was not found, because God had translated him: for before his translation he had this testimony, that he pleased God.
But without faith it is impossible to please him: for he that cometh to God must believe that he is, and that he is a rewarder of them that diligently seek him.
By faith Noah, being warned of God of things not seen as yet, moved with fear, prepared an ark to the saving of his house; by the which he condemned the world, and became heir of the righteousness which is by faith.
By faith Abraham, when he was called to go out into a place which he should after receive for an inher-

itance, obeyed; and he went out, not knowing whither he went.

By faith he sojourned in the land of promise, as in a strange country, dwelling in tabernacles with Isaac and Jacob, the heirs with him of the same promise;

For he looked for a city which hath foundations, whose builder and maker is God.

Through faith also Sara herself received strength to conceive seed, and was delivered of a child when she was past age, because she judged him faithful who had promised.

Therefore sprang there even of one, and him as good as dead, so many as the stars of the sky in multitude, and as the sand which is by the seashore innumerable.

These all died in faith, not having received the promises, but having seen them afar off, and were persuaded of them, and embraced them, and confessed that they were strangers and pilgrims on the earth.

For they that say such things declare plainly that they seek a country.

And truly, if they had been mindful of that country from whence they came out, they might have had opportunity to have returned.

But now they desire a better country, that is, a heavenly: wherefore God is not ashamed to be called their God: for he hath prepared for them a city.

By faith Abraham, when he was tried, offered up Isaac: and he that had received the promises offered up his only begotten son.

Of whom it was said, That in Isaac shall thy seed be called:

Accounting that God was able to raise him up, even

from the dead; from whence also he received him
in a figure.

By faith Isaac blessed Jacob and Esau concerning
things to come.

By faith Jacob, when he was a dying, blessed both the
sons of Joseph; and worshipped, leaning upon the
top of his staff.

By faith Joseph, when he died, made mention of the
departing of the children of Israel; and gave commandment concerning his bones.

By faith Moses, when he was born, was hid three
months of his parents, because they saw he was a
proper child; and they were not afraid of the king's
commandment.

By faith Moses, when he was come to years, refused to
be called the son of Pharaoh's daughter;

Choosing rather to suffer affliction with the people
of God, than to enjoy the pleasures of sin for a
season;

Esteeming the reproach of Christ greater riches than
the treasures in Egypt: for he had respect unto the
recompense of the reward.

By faith he forsook Egypt, not fearing the wrath of
the king: for he endured, as seeing him who is
invisible.

Through faith he kept the passover, and the sprinkling
of blood, lest he that destroyed the firstborn should
touch them.

By faith they passed through the Red Sea as by dry
land: which the Egyptians assaying to do were
drowned.

By faith the walls of Jericho fell down, after they were
compassed about seven days.

By faith the harlot Rahab perished not with them that

believed not, when she had received the spies with peace.

And what shall I more say? For the time would fail me to tell of Gedeon, and of Barak, and of Samson, and of Jephthae; of David also, and Samuel, and of the prophets,

Who through faith subdued kingdoms, wrought righteousness, obtained promises, stopped the mouths of lions,

Quenched the violence of fire, escaped the edge of the sword, out of weakness were made strong, waxed valiant in fight, turned to flight the armies of the aliens.

Women received their dead raised to life again: and others were tortured, not accepting deliverance; that they might obtain a better resurrection:

And others had trial of cruel mockings and scourgings, yea, moreover of bonds and imprisonment:

They were stoned, they were sawn asunder, were tempted, were slain with the sword: they wandered about in sheepskins and goatskins; being destitute, afflicted, tormented;

(Of whom the world was not worthy); they wandered in deserts, and in mountains, and in dens and caves of the earth.

And these all, having obtained a good report through faith, received not the promise:

God having provided some better thing for us, that they without us should not be made perfect.

HEBREWS 11:1-40

That the trial of your faith, being much more precious than of gold that perisheth, though it be tried with fire, might be found unto praise and honour and glory at the appearing of Jesus Christ:

Whom having not seen, ye love; in whom, though now ye see him not, yet believing, ye rejoice with joy unspeakable and full of glory:

Receiving the end of your faith, even the salvation of your souls.

1 PETER 1:7-9

For whatsoever is born of God overcometh the world: and this is the victory that overcometh the world, even our faith.

1 JOHN 5:4

Fear none of those things which thou shalt suffer: behold, the devil shall cast some of you into prison, that ye may be tried; and ye shall have tribulation ten days: be thou faithful unto death, and I will give thee a crown of life.

REVELATION 2:10

LOVE

And Jacob served seven years for Rachel; and they seemed unto him but a few days, for the love he had to her.

GENESIS 29:20

Thou shalt not avenge, nor bear any grudge against the children of thy people, but thou shalt love thy neighbour as thyself: I am the Lord.

LEVITICUS 19:18

But the stranger that dwelleth with you shall be unto you as one born among you, and thou shalt love him as thyself; for ye were strangers in the land of Egypt: I am the Lord your God.

LEVITICUS 19:34

Thou shalt have none other gods before me. Thou shalt not make thee any graven image, or any likeness of any thing that is in heaven above, or that is in the earth beneath, or that is in the waters beneath the earth:
Thou shalt not bow down thyself unto them, nor serve them: for I the Lord thy God am a jealous God, visiting the iniquity of the fathers upon the children

unto the third and fourth generation of them that hate me,

And showing mercy unto thousands of them that love me and keep my commandments.

DEUTERONOMY 5:7-10

And thou shalt love the Lord thy God with all thine heart, and with all thy soul, and with all thy might.

DEUTERONOMY 6:5

For thou art a holy people unto the Lord thy God: the Lord thy God hath chosen thee to be a special people unto himself, above all people that are upon the face of the earth.

The Lord did not set his love upon you, nor choose you, because ye were more in number than any people; for ye were the fewest of all people:

But because the Lord loved you, and because he would keep the oath which he had sworn unto your fathers, hath the Lord brought you out with a mighty hand, and redeemed you out of the house of bondmen, from the hand of Pharaoh king of Egypt.

Know therefore that the Lord thy God, he is God, the faithful God, which keepeth covenant and mercy with them that love him and keep his commandments to a thousand generations;

And repayeth them that hate him to their face, to

destroy them: he will not be slack to him that
hateth him, he will repay him to his face.
Thou shalt therefore keep the commandments, and
the statutes, and the judgments, which I command
thee this day, to do them.

DEUTERONOMY 7:6-11

I am distressed for thee, my brother Jonathan:
very pleasant hast thou been unto me: thy
love to me was wonderful, passing the love of
women.

2 SAMUEL 1:26

O ye sons of men, how long will ye turn my
glory into shame? How long will ye love vanity, and seek after leasing? Selah.

PSALM 4:2

But let all those that put their trust in thee
rejoice: let them ever shout for joy, because
thou defendest them: let them also that love
thy name be joyful in thee.

PSALM 5:11

The seed also of his servants shall inherit it: and they that love his name shall dwell therein.

PSALM 69:36

Because he hath set his love upon me, therefore will I deliver him: I will set him on high, because he hath known my name.

PSALM 91:14

Ye that love the Lord, hate evil: he preserveth the souls of his saints; he delivereth them out of the hand of the wicked.

PSALM 97:10

Many are my persecutors and mine enemies; yet do I not decline from thy testimonies.
I beheld the transgressors, and was grieved; because they kept not thy word.
Consider how I love thy precepts: quicken me, O Lord, according to thy loving-kindness.
Thy word is true from the beginning: and every one of thy righteous judgments endureth forever.

PSALM 119:157-160

Hear, ye children, the instruction of a father, and attend to know understanding. For I give you good doctrine, forsake ye not my law.

For I was my father's son, tender and only beloved in the sight of my mother.

He taught me also, and said unto me, Let thine heart retain my words: keep my commandments, and live.

Get wisdom, get understanding: forget it not; neither decline from the words of my mouth.

Forsake her not, and she shall preserve thee: love her, and she shall keep thee.

Wisdom is the principal thing; therefore get wisdom: and with all thy getting get understanding.

Exalt her, and she shall promote thee: she shall bring thee to honour, when thou dost embrace her.

She shall give to thine head an ornament of grace: a crown of glory shall she deliver to thee.

PROVERBS 4:1-9

Let thy fountain be blessed: and rejoice with the wife of thy youth. Let her be as the loving hind and pleasant roe; let her breasts satisfy thee at all times; and be thou ravished always with her love.

PROVERBS 5:18-19

I wisdom dwell with prudence, and find out knowledge of witty inventions.

The fear of the Lord is to hate evil: pride, and arrogancy, and the evil way, and the froward mouth, do I hate.

Counsel is mine, and sound wisdom: I am understanding; I have strength.

By me kings reign, and princes decree justice.

By me princes rule, and nobles, even all the judges of the earth.

I love them that love me; and those that seek me early shall find me.

Riches and honour are with me; yea, durable riches and righteousness.

My fruit is better than gold, yea, than fine gold; and my revenue than choice silver.

I lead in the way of righteousness, in the midst of the paths of judgment:

That I may cause those that love me to inherit substance; and I will fill their treasures.

The Lord possessed me in the beginning of his way, before his works of old.

I was set up from everlasting, from the beginning, or ever the earth was.

When there were no depths, I was brought forth; when there were no fountains abounding with water.

Before the mountains were settled, before the hills was I brought forth:

While as yet he had not made the earth, nor the fields, nor the highest part of the dust of the world.

When he prepared the heavens, I was there: when he set a compass upon the face of the depth:

When he established the clouds above: when he strengthened the fountains of the deep:

When he gave to the sea his decree, that the waters
should not pass his commandment: when he
appointed the foundations of the earth:
Then I was by him, as one brought up with him: and
I was daily his delight, rejoicing always before
him;
Rejoicing in the habitable part of his earth; and my
delights were with the sons of men.

PROVERBS 8:12-31

Reprove not a scorner, lest he hate thee: rebuke
a wise man, and he will love thee.
Give instruction to a wise man, and he will
be yet wiser: teach a just man, and he will increase
in learning.
The fear of the Lord is the beginning of wisdom: and
the knowledge of the holy is understanding.

PROVERBS 9:9-10

Hatred stirreth up strifes: but love covereth all
sins.
In the lips of him that hath understanding
wisdom is found: but a rod is for the back of him
that is void of understanding.
Wise men lay up knowledge: but the mouth of the
foolish is near destruction.
The rich man's wealth is his strong city: the destruction of the poor is their poverty.

The labour of the righteous tendeth to life: the fruit of
the wicked to sin.

PROVERBS 10:12-16

The heart of him that hath understanding
seeketh knowledge: but the mouth of fools
feedeth on foolishness.
All the days of the afflicted are evil: but he that is of a
merry heart hath a continual feast.
Better is little with the fear of the Lord than great trea-
sure and trouble therewith.
Better is a dinner of herbs where love is, than a stalled
ox and hatred therewith.

PROVERBS 15:14-17

Righteous lips are the delight of kings; and
they love him that speaketh right.

PROVERBS 16:13

Death and life are in the power of the tongue:
and they that love it shall eat the fruit thereof.
Whoso findeth a wife findeth a good thing, and
obtaineth favour of the Lord.

PROVERBS 18:21-22

A good name is rather to be chosen than great riches, and loving favour rather than silver and gold.

PROVERBS 22:1

A time to love, and a time to hate; a time of war, and a time of peace.

ECCLESIASTES 3:8

Let him kiss me with the kisses of his mouth: for thy love is better than wine.
Because of the savour of thy good ointments thy name is as ointment poured forth, therefore do the virgins love thee.

Draw me, we will run after thee: the king hath brought me into his chambers: we will be glad and rejoice in thee, we will remember thy love more than wine: the upright love thee.

I am black, but comely, O ye daughters of Jerusalem, as the tents of Kedar, as the curtains of Solomon.

Look not upon me, because I am black, because the sun hath looked upon me: my mother's children were angry with me; they made me the keeper of the vineyards; but mine own vineyard have I not kept.

Tell me, O thou whom my soul loveth, where thou feedest, where thou makest thy flock to rest at noon: for why should I be as one that turneth aside by the flocks of thy companions?

If thou know not, O thou fairest among women, go thy way forth by the footsteps of the flock, and feed thy kids beside the shepherds' tents.

I have compared thee, O my love, to a company of horses in Pharaoh's chariots.

Thy cheeks are comely with rows of jewels, thy neck with chains of gold.

We will make thee borders of gold with studs of silver.

While the king sitteth at his table, my spikenard sendeth forth the smell thereof.

A bundle of myrrh is my well-beloved unto me; he shall lie all night betwixt my breasts.

My beloved is unto me as a cluster of camphire in the vineyards of Engedi.

Behold, thou art fair, my love; behold, thou art fair; thou hast doves' eyes.

Behold, thou art fair, my beloved, yea, pleasant: also our bed is green.

The beams of our house are cedar, and our rafters of fir.

SONG OF SOLOMON 1:1-17

I am the rose of Sharon, and the lily of the valleys.

As the lily among thorns, so is my love among the daughters.

As the apple tree among the trees of the wood, so is my beloved among the sons. I sat down under his shadow with great delight, and his fruit was sweet to my taste.

He brought me to the banqueting house, and his banner over me was love.

Stay me with flagons, comfort me with apples: for I am sick of love.

His left hand is under my head, and his right hand
   doth embrace me.
I charge you, O ye daughters of Jerusalem, by the roes,
   and by the hinds of the field, that ye stir not up,
   nor awake my love, till he please.
The voice of my beloved! Behold, he cometh leaping
   upon the mountains, skipping upon the hills.
My beloved is like a roe or a young hart: behold, he
   standeth behind our wall, he looketh forth at the
   windows, showing himself through the lattice.
My beloved spake, and said unto me, Rise up, my love,
   my fair one, and come away.
For, lo, the winter is past, the rain is over and gone;
The flowers appear on the earth; the time of the
   singing of birds is come, and the voice of the tur-
   tle is heard in our land;
The fig tree putteth forth her green figs, and the vines
   with the tender grape give a good smell. Arise, my
   love, my fair one, and come away.

SONG OF SOLOMON 2:1-13

By night on my bed I sought him whom my
soul loveth: I sought him, but I found him
not.
I will rise now, and go about the city in the streets,
and in the broad ways I will seek him whom my
soul loveth: I sought him, but I found him not.

SONG OF SOLOMON 3:1-2

ehold, thou art fair, my love; behold, thou art fair; thou hast doves' eyes within thy locks: thy hair is as a flock of goats, that appear from mount Gilead.

Thy teeth are like a flock of sheep that are even shorn, which came up from the washing; whereof everyone bear twins, and none is barren among them.

Thy lips are like a thread of scarlet, and thy speech is comely: thy temples are like a piece of a pomegranate within thy locks.

Thy neck is like the tower of David builded for an armoury, whereon there hang a thousand bucklers, all shields of mighty men.

Thy two breasts are like two young roes that are twins, which feed among the lilies.

Until the day break, and the shadows flee away, I will get me to the mountain of myrrh, and to the hill of frankincense.

Thou art all fair, my love; there is no spot in thee.

Come with me from Lebanon, my spouse, with me from Lebanon: look from the top of Amana, from the top of Shenir and Hermon, from the lions' dens, from the mountains of the leopards.

Thou hast ravished my heart, my sister, my spouse; thou hast ravished my heart with one of thine eyes, with one chain of thy neck.

How fair is thy love, my sister, my spouse! how much better is thy love than wine! and the smell of thine ointments than all spices!

Thy lips, O my spouse, drop as the honeycomb: honey and milk are under thy tongue; and the smell of thy garments is like the smell of Lebanon.

A garden enclosed is my sister, my spouse; a spring shut up, a fountain sealed.

Thy plants are an orchard of pomegranates, with

pleasant fruits; camphire, with spikenard,

Spikenard and saffron; calamus and cinnamon, with all trees of frankincense; myrrh and aloes, with all the chief spices:

A fountain of gardens, a well of living waters, and streams from Lebanon.

Awake, O north wind; and come, thou south; blow upon my garden, that the spices thereof may flow out. Let my beloved come into his garden, and eat his pleasant fruits.

SONG OF SOLOMON 4:1-16

I am come into my garden, my sister, my spouse: I have gathered my myrrh with my spice; I have eaten my honeycomb with my honey; I have drunk my wine with my milk: eat, O friends; drink, yea, drink abundantly, O beloved.

I sleep, but my heart waketh: it is the voice of my beloved that knocketh, saying, Open to me, my sister, my love, my dove, my undefiled: for my head is filled with dew, and my locks with the drops of the night.

I have put off my coat; how shall I put it on? I have washed my feet; how shall I defile them?

My beloved put in his hand by the hole of the door, and my bowels were moved for him.

I rose up to open to my beloved; and my hands dropped with myrrh, and my fingers with sweet smelling myrrh, upon the handles of the lock.

I opened to my beloved; but my beloved had withdrawn himself, and was gone: my soul failed when he spake: I sought him, but I could not find him; I called him, but he gave me no answer.

The watchmen that went about the city found me, they smote me, they wounded me; the keepers of the walls took away my veil from me.

I charge you, O daughters of Jerusalem, if ye find my beloved, that ye tell him, that I am sick of love.

What is thy beloved more than another beloved, O thou fairest among women? what is thy beloved more than another beloved, that thou dost so charge us?

My beloved is white and ruddy, the chiefest among ten thousand.

His head is as the most fine gold, his locks are bushy, and black as a raven.

His eyes are as the eyes of doves by the rivers of waters, washed with milk, and fitly set.

His cheeks are as a bed of spices, as sweet flowers: his lips like lilies, dropping sweet smelling myrrh.

His hands are as gold rings set with the beryl: his belly is as bright ivory overlaid with sapphires.

His legs are as pillars of marble, set upon sockets of fine gold: his countenance is as Lebanon, excellent as the cedars.

His mouth is most sweet: yea, he is altogether lovely. This is my beloved, and this is my friend, O daughters of Jerusalem.

SONG OF SOLOMON 5:1-16

Whither is thy beloved gone, O thou fairest among women? whither is thy beloved turned aside? that we may seek him with thee.

My beloved is gone down into his garden, to the beds of spices, to feed in the gardens, and to gather lilies.

I am my beloved's, and my beloved is mine: he feedeth among the lilies.

Thou art beautiful, O my love, as Tirzah, comely as Jerusalem, terrible as an army with banners.

Turn away thine eyes from me, for they have overcome me: thy hair is as a flock of goats that appear from Gilead.

Thy teeth are as a flock of sheep which go up from the washing, whereof every one beareth twins, and there is not one barren among them.

As a piece of a pomegranate are thy temples within thy locks.

There are threescore queens, and fourscore concubines, and virgins without number.

My dove, my undefiled is but one; she is the only one of her mother, she is the choice one of her that bore her. The daughters saw her, and blessed her; yea, the queens and the concubines, and they praised her.

Who is she that looketh forth as the morning, fair as the moon, clear as the sun, and terrible as an army with banners?

SONG OF SOLOMON 6:1-10

How beautiful are thy feet with shoes, O prince's daughter! the joints of thy thighs are like jewels, the work of the hands of a cunning workman.

Thy navel is like a round goblet, which wanteth not liquor: thy belly is like a heap of wheat set about with lilies.

Thy two breasts are like two young roes that are twins.

Thy neck is as a tower of ivory; thine eyes like the fish-pools in Heshbon, by the gate of Bathrabbim: thy nose is as the tower of Lebanon which looketh toward Damascus.

Thine head upon thee is like Carmel, and the hair of thine head like purple; the king is held in the galleries.

How fair and how pleasant art thou, O love, for delights!

This thy stature is like to a palm tree, and thy breasts to clusters of grapes.

I said, I will go up to the palm tree, I will take hold of the boughs thereof: now also thy breasts shall be as clusters of the vine, and the smell of thy nose like apples;

And the roof of thy mouth like the best wine for my beloved, that goeth down sweetly, causing the lips of those that are asleep to speak.

I am my beloved's, and his desire is toward me.

Come, my beloved, let us go forth into the field; let us lodge in the villages.

Let us get up early to the vineyards; let us see if the vine flourish, whether the tender grape appear, and the pomegranates bud forth: there will I give thee my loves.

The mandrakes give a smell, and at our gates are all

manner of pleasant fruits, new and old, which I
have laid up for thee, O my beloved.

SONG OF SOLOMON 7:1-13

O that thou wert as my brother, that sucked the
breasts of my mother! when I should find
thee without, I would kiss thee; yea, I should
not be despised.
I would lead thee, and bring thee into my mother's
house, who would instruct me: I would cause thee
to drink of spiced wine of the juice of my pomegranate.
His left hand should be under my head, and his right
hand should embrace me.
I charge you, O daughters of Jerusalem, that ye stir not
up, nor awake my love, until he please.
Who is this that cometh up from the wilderness, leaning upon her beloved? I raised thee up under the
apple tree: there thy mother brought thee forth:
there she brought thee forth that bore thee.
Set me as a seal upon thine heart, as a seal upon thine
arm: for love is strong as death; jealousy is cruel as
the grave: the coals thereof are coals of fire, which
hath a most vehement flame.
Many waters cannot quench love, neither can the
floods drown it: if a man would give all the substance of his house for love, it would utterly be
contemned.
We have a little sister, and she hath no breasts: what
shall we do for our sister in the day when she
shall be spoken for?
If she be a wall, we will build upon her a palace of sil-

ver: and if she be a door, we will enclose her with boards of cedar.

I am a wall, and my breasts like towers: then was I in his eyes as one that found favour.

Solomon had a vineyard at Baalhamon; he let out the vineyard unto keepers; every one for the fruit thereof was to bring a thousand pieces of silver.

My vineyard, which is mine, is before me: thou, O Solomon, must have a thousand, and those that keep the fruit thereof two hundred.

Thou that dwellest in the gardens, the companions hearken to thy voice: cause me to hear it.

Make haste, my beloved, and be thou like to a roe or to a young hart upon the mountains of spices.

SONG OF SOLOMON 8:1-14

I will heal their backsliding, I will love them freely: for mine anger is turned away from him.

I will be as the dew unto Israel: he shall grow as the lily, and cast forth his roots as Lebanon.

His branches shall spread, and his beauty shall be as the olive tree, and his smell as Lebanon.

They that dwell under his shadow shall return; they shall revive as the corn, and grow as the vine: the scent thereof shall be as the wine of Lebanon.

HOSEA 14:4-7

Wherewith shall I come before the Lord, and bow myself before the high God? shall I come before him with burnt offerings, with calves of a year old?

Will the Lord be pleased with thousands of rams, or with ten thousands of rivers of oil? shall I give my firstborn for my transgression, the fruit of my body for the sin of my soul?

He hath showed thee, O man, what is good; and what doth the Lord require of thee, but to do justly, and to love mercy, and to walk humbly with thy God?

The Lord's voice crieth unto the city, and the man of wisdom shall see thy name: hear ye the rod, and who hath appointed it.

MICAH 6:6-9

Ye have heard that it hath been said, Thou shalt love thy neighbour, and hate thine enemy.

But I say unto you, Love your enemies, bless them that curse you; do good to them that hate you, and pray for them which despitefully use you, and persecute you;

That ye may be the children of your Father which is in heaven: for he maketh his sun to rise on the evil and on the good, and sendeth rain on the just and on the unjust.

For if ye love them which love you, what reward have ye? do not even the publicans the same?

And if ye salute your brethren only, what do ye more than others? do not even the publicans so?

Be ye therefore perfect, even as your Father which is in heaven is perfect.

MATTHEW 5:43-48

Honour thy father and thy mother: and, Thou shalt love thy neighbour as thyself.

MATTHEW 19:19

Jesus said unto him, Thou shalt love the Lord thy God with all thy heart, and with all thy soul, and with all thy mind.
This is the first and great commandment.
And the second is like unto it, Thou shalt love thy neighbour as thyself.
On these two commandments hang all the law and the prophets.

MATTHEW 22:37–40

And Jesus answered him, The first of all the commandments is, Hear, O Israel; The Lord our God is one Lord:
And thou shalt love the Lord thy God with all thy heart, and with all thy soul, and with all thy mind, and with all thy strength: this is the first commandment.
And the second is like, namely this, Thou shalt love thy neighbour as thyself. There is none other commandment greater than these.

MARK 12:29–31

But I say unto you which hear, Love your enemies, do good to them which hate you,
Bless them that curse you, and pray for them which despitefully use you.

And unto him that smiteth thee on the one cheek offer also the other; and him that taketh away thy cloak forbid not to take thy coat also.

Give to every man that asketh of thee; and of him that taketh away thy goods ask them not again.

And as ye would that men should do to you, do ye also to them likewise.

For if ye love them which love you, what thank have ye? for sinners also love those that love them.

And if ye do good to them which do good to you, what thank have ye? for sinners also do even the same.

And if ye lend to them of whom ye hope to receive, what thank have ye? for sinners also lend to sinners, to receive as much again.

But love ye your enemies, and do good, and lend, hoping for nothing again; and your reward shall be great, and ye shall be the children of the Highest: for he is kind unto the unthankful and to the evil.

Be ye therefore merciful, as your Father also is merciful.

Judge not, and ye shall not be judged: condemn not, and ye shall not be condemned: forgive, and ye shall be forgiven:

Give, and it shall be given unto you; good measure, pressed down, and shaken together, and running over, shall men give into your bosom. For with the same measure that ye mete withal it shall be measured to you again.

And he spake a parable unto them, Can the blind lead the blind? shall they not both fall into the ditch?

The disciple is not above his master: but everyone that is perfect shall be as his master.

LUKE 6:27–40

There was a certain creditor which had two debtors: the one owed five hundred pence, and the other fifty.

And when they had nothing to pay, he frankly forgave them both. Tell me therefore, which of them will love him most?

Simon answered and said, I suppose that he, to whom he forgave most. And he said unto him, Thou hast rightly judged.

And he turned to the woman, and said unto Simon, Seest thou this woman? I entered into thine house, thou gavest me no water for my feet: but she hath washed my feet with tears, and wiped them with the hairs of her head.

Thou gavest me no kiss: but this woman since the time I came in hath not ceased to kiss my feet.

My head with oil thou didst not anoint: but this woman hath anointed my feet with ointment.

Wherefore I say unto thee, Her sins, which are many, are forgiven; for she loved much: but to whom little is forgiven, the same loveth little.

And he said unto her, Thy sins are forgiven.

LUKE 7:41–48

Ye fools, did not he that made that which is without make that which is within also? But rather give alms of such things as ye have; and, behold, all things are clean unto you.

But woe unto you, Pharisees! for ye tithe mint and rue and all manner of herbs, and pass over judgment and the love of God: these ought ye to have done, and not to leave the other undone.

Woe unto you, Pharisees! for ye love the uppermost seats in the synagogues, and greetings in the markets.

Woe unto you, scribes and Pharisees, hypocrites! for ye are as graves which appear not, and the men that walk over them are not aware of them.

LUKE 11:40–44

No servant can serve two masters: for either he will hate the one, and love the other; or else he will hold to the one, and despise the other. Ye cannot serve God and mammon.

LUKE 16:13

Jesus said unto them, If God were your Father, ye would love me: for I proceeded forth and came from God; neither came I of myself, but he sent me.

JOHN 8:42

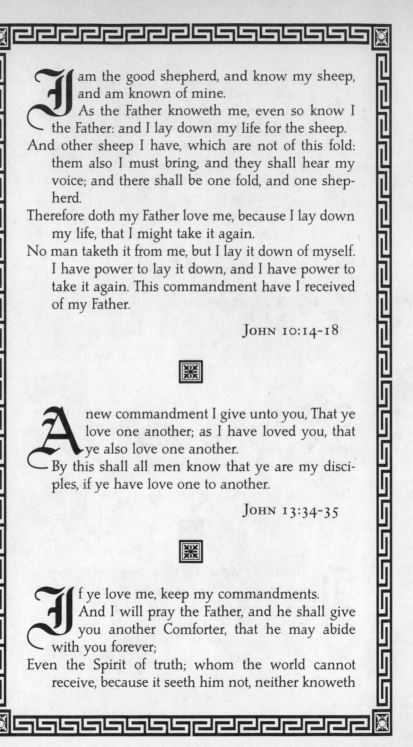

I am the good shepherd, and know my sheep, and am known of mine.

As the Father knoweth me, even so know I the Father: and I lay down my life for the sheep.

And other sheep I have, which are not of this fold: them also I must bring, and they shall hear my voice; and there shall be one fold, and one shepherd.

Therefore doth my Father love me, because I lay down my life, that I might take it again.

No man taketh it from me, but I lay it down of myself. I have power to lay it down, and I have power to take it again. This commandment have I received of my Father.

JOHN 10:14-18

A new commandment I give unto you, That ye love one another; as I have loved you, that ye also love one another.

By this shall all men know that ye are my disciples, if ye have love one to another.

JOHN 13:34-35

If ye love me, keep my commandments.

And I will pray the Father, and he shall give you another Comforter, that he may abide with you forever;

Even the Spirit of truth; whom the world cannot receive, because it seeth him not, neither knoweth

him: but ye know him; for he dwelleth with you, and shall be in you.

I will not leave you comfortless: I will come to you.

Yet a little while, and the world seeth me no more; but ye see me: because I live, ye shall live also.

At that day ye shall know that I am in my Father, and ye in me, and I in you.

He that hath my commandments, and keepeth them, he it is that loveth me: and he that loveth me shall be loved of my Father, and I will love him, and will manifest myself to him.

JOHN 14:15-21

This is my commandment, That ye love one another, as I have loved you.

Greater love hath no man than this, that a man lay down his life for his friends.

Ye are my friends, if ye do whatsoever I command you.

Henceforth I call you not servants; for the servant knoweth not what his lord doeth: but I have called you friends; for all things that I have heard of my Father I have made known unto you.

Ye have not chosen me, but I have chosen you, and ordained you, that ye should go and bring forth fruit, and that your fruit should remain: that whatsoever ye shall ask of the Father in my name, he may give it you.

These things I command you, that ye love one another.

JOHN 15:12-17

Who shall separate us from the love of Christ? shall tribulation, or distress, or persecution, or famine, or nakedness, or peril, or sword? As it is written, For thy sake we are killed all the day long; we are accounted as sheep for the slaughter.

Nay, in all these things we are more than conquerors through him that loved us.

For I am persuaded, that neither death, nor life, nor angels, nor principalities, nor powers, nor things present, nor things to come,

Nor height, nor depth, nor any other creature, shall be able to separate us from the love of God, which is in Christ Jesus our Lord.

ROMANS 8:35-39

Be kindly affectioned one to another with brotherly love; in honour preferring one another;

Not slothful in business; fervent in spirit; serving the Lord;

Rejoicing in hope; patient in tribulation; continuing instant in prayer;

Distributing to the necessity of saints; given to hospitality.

Bless them which persecute you: bless, and curse not.

Rejoice with them that do rejoice, and weep with them that weep.

Be of the same mind one toward another. Mind not high things, but condescend to men of low estate. Be not wise in your own conceits.

Recompense to no man evil for evil. Provide things honest in the sight of all men.

If it be possible, as much as lieth in you, live peaceably
with all men.
Dearly beloved, avenge not yourselves, but rather give
place unto wrath: for it is written, Vengeance is
mine; I will repay, saith the Lord.

ROMANS 12:10-19

Owe no man anything, but to love one another: for he that loveth another hath fulfilled
the law.
For this, Thou shalt not commit adultery, Thou shalt
not kill, Thou shalt not steal, Thou shalt not bear
false witness, Thou shalt not covet; and if there be
any other commandment, it is briefly compre-
hended in this saying, namely, Thou shalt love thy
neighbour as thyself.
Love worketh no ill to his neighbour: therefore love is
the fulfilling of the law.

ROMANS 13:8-10

But as it is written, Eye hath not seen, nor ear
heard, neither have entered into the heart of
man, the things which God hath prepared for
them that love him.

1 CORINTHIANS 2:9

For, brethren, ye have been called unto liberty; only use not liberty for an occasion to the flesh, but by love serve one another.

For all the law is fulfilled in one word, even in this; Thou shalt love thy neighbour as thyself.

GALATIANS 5:13-14

Husbands, love your wives, even as Christ also loved the church, and gave himself for it;

That he might sanctify and cleanse it with the washing of water by the word,

That he might present it to himself a glorious church, not having spot, or wrinkle, or any such thing; but that it should be holy and without blemish.

So ought men to love their wives as their own bodies. He that loveth his wife loveth himself.

EPHESIANS 5:25-28

If there be therefore any consolation in Christ, if any comfort of love, if any fellowship of the Spirit, if any bowels and mercies,

Fulfill ye my joy, that ye be likeminded, having the same love, being of one accord, of one mind.

Let nothing be done through strife or vainglory; but in lowliness of mind let each esteem other better than themselves.

Look not every man on his own things, but every man also on the things of others.

Let this mind be in you, which was also in Christ Jesus:

Who, being in the form of God, thought it not robbery
to be equal with God:

But made himself of no reputation, and took upon him
the form of a servant, and was made in the likeness of men:

And being found in fashion as a man, he humbled
himself, and became obedient unto death, even
the death of the cross.

Wherefore God also hath highly exalted him, and
given him a name which is above every name:

That at the name of Jesus every knee should bow, of
things in heaven, and things in earth, and things
under the earth;

And that every tongue should confess that Jesus
Christ is Lord, to the glory of God the Father.

Wherefore, my beloved, as ye have always obeyed,
not as in my presence only, but now much more
in my absence, work out your own salvation with
fear and trembling.

For it is God which worketh in you both to will and to
do of his good pleasure.

PHILIPPIANS 2:1-13

And whatsoever ye do in word or deed, do all
in the name of the Lord Jesus, giving thanks
to God and the Father by him.

Wives, submit yourselves unto your own husbands, as it is fit in the Lord.

Husbands, love your wives, and be not bitter against
them.

Children, obey your parents in all things: for this is
well pleasing unto the Lord.

Fathers, provoke not your children to anger, lest they
be discouraged.

Servants, obey in all things your masters according to
the flesh; not with eyeservice, as men-pleasers; but
in singleness of heart, fearing God:

And whatsoever ye do, do it heartily, as to the Lord,
and not unto men;

Knowing that of the Lord ye shall receive the reward
of the inheritance: for ye serve the Lord Christ.

But he that doeth wrong shall receive for the wrong
which he hath done: and there is no respect of
persons.

COLOSSIANS 3:17-25

But let us, who are of the day, be sober, putting
on the breastplate of faith and love; and for a
helmet, the hope of salvation.

For God hath not appointed us to wrath, but to
obtain salvation by our Lord Jesus Christ,

Who died for us, that, whether we wake or sleep, we
should live together with him.

1 THESSALONIANS 5:8-10

I have fought a good fight, I have finished my
course, I have kept the faith:

Henceforth there is laid up for me a crown of
righteousness, which the Lord, the righteous judge,
shall give me at that day: and not to me only, but
unto all them also that love his appearing.

2 TIMOTHY 4:7-8

et brotherly love continue.
Be not forgetful to entertain strangers: for thereby some have entertained angels unawares.

HEBREWS 13:1-2

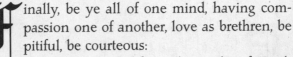

lessed is the man that endureth temptation: for when he is tried, he shall receive the crown of life, which the Lord hath promised to them that love him.

JAMES 1:12

inally, be ye all of one mind, having compassion one of another, love as brethren, be pitiful, be courteous:
Not rendering evil for evil, or railing for railing: but contrariwise blessing; knowing that ye are thereunto called, that ye should inherit a blessing.
For he that will love life, and see good days, let him refrain his tongue from evil, and his lips that they speak no guile:
Let him eschew evil, and do good; let him seek peace, and pursue it.

1 PETER 3:8-11

But whoso keepeth his word, in him verily is the love of God perfected: hereby know we that we are in him.

1 JOHN 2:5

Love not the world, neither the things that are in the world. If any man love the world, the love of the Father is not in him.
For all that is in the world, the lust of the flesh, and the lust of the eyes, and the pride of life, is not of the Father, but is of the world.

1 JOHN 2:15-16

Hereby perceive we the love of God, because he laid down his life for us: and we ought to lay down our lives for the brethren.
But whoso hath this world's good, and seeth his brother have need, and shutteth up his bowels of compassion from him, how dwelleth the love of God in him?
My little children, let us not love in word, neither in tongue; but in deed and in truth.

1 JOHN 3:16-18

eloved, let us love one another: for love is of
God; and every one that loveth is born of
God, and knoweth God.
He that loveth not knoweth not God; for God is
love.

1 JOHN 4:7-8

erein is love, not that we loved God, but that
he loved us, and sent his Son to be the pro-
pitiation for our sins.
Beloved, if God so loved us, we ought also to love
one another.
No man hath seen God at any time. If we love one
another, God dwelleth in us, and his love is perfected in us.
Hereby know we that we dwell in him, and he in us,
because he hath given us of his Spirit.
And we have seen and do testify that the Father sent
the Son to be the Saviour of the world.
Whosoever shall confess that Jesus is the Son of God,
God dwelleth in him, and he in God.
And we have known and believed the love that God
hath to us. God is love; and he that dwelleth in
love dwelleth in God, and God in him.
Herein is our love made perfect, that we may have
boldness in the day of judgment: because as he is,
so are we in this world.
There is no fear in love; but perfect love casteth out
fear: because fear hath torment. He that feareth is
not made perfect in love.
We love him, because he first loved us.
If a man say, I love God, and hateth his brother, he is

a liar: for he that loveth not his brother whom he
hath seen, how can he love God whom he hath
not seen?
And this commandment have we from him, That he
who loveth God love his brother also.

1 JOHN 4:10-21

HOPE

Even that it would please God to destroy me; that he would let loose his hand, and cut me off!

Then should I yet have comfort; yea, I would harden myself in sorrow: let him not spare; for I have not concealed the words of the Holy One.

What is my strength, that I should hope? and what is mine end, that I should prolong my life?

JOB 6:9-11

My flesh is clothed with worms and clods of dust; my skin is broken, and become loathsome.

My days are swifter than a weaver's shuttle, and are spent without hope.

O remember that my life is wind: mine eye shall no more see good.

JOB 7:5-7

Can the rush grow up without mire? can the flag grow without water?

Whilst it is yet in his greenness, and not cut down, it withereth before any other herb.

So are the paths of all that forget God; and the hypocrite's hope shall perish:

Whose hope shall be cut off, and whose trust shall be a spider's web.

He shall lean upon his house, but it shall not stand: he
shall hold it fast, but it shall not endure.

JOB 8:11-15

If thou prepare thine heart, and stretch out
thine hands toward him;
If iniquity be in thine hand, put it far away,
and let not wickedness dwell in thy tabernacles.
For then shalt thou lift up thy face without spot; yea,
thou shalt be steadfast, and shalt not fear:
Because thou shalt forget thy misery, and remember it
as waters that pass away:
And thine age shall be clearer than the noonday; thou
shalt shine forth, thou shalt be as the morning.
And thou shalt be secure, because there is hope; yea,
thou shalt dig about thee, and thou shalt take thy
rest in safety.
Also thou shalt lie down, and none shall make thee
afraid; yea, many shall make suit unto thee.
But the eyes of the wicked shall fail, and they shall not
escape, and their hope shall be as the giving up of
the ghost.

JOB 11:13-20

For there is hope of a tree, if it be cut down,
that it will sprout again, and that the tender
branch thereof will not cease.

JOB 14:7

If I wait, the grave is mine house: I have made my bed in the darkness.

I have said to corruption, Thou art my father: to the worm, Thou art my mother, and my sister.

And where is now my hope? as for my hope, who shall see it?

They shall go down to the bars of the pit, when our rest together is in the dust.

JOB 17:13-16

For what is the hope of the hypocrite, though he hath gained, when God taketh away his soul?

JOB 27:8

The Lord is the portion of mine inheritance and of my cup: thou maintainest my lot.

The lines are fallen unto me in pleasant places; yea, I have a goodly heritage.

I will bless the Lord, who hath given me counsel: my reins also instruct me in the night seasons.

I have set the Lord always before me: because he is at my right hand, I shall not be moved.

Therefore my heart is glad, and my glory rejoiceth: my flesh also shall rest in hope.

For thou wilt not leave my soul in hell; neither wilt thou suffer thine Holy One to see corruption.

Thou wilt show me the path of life: in thy presence is

fulness of joy; at thy right hand there are pleasures forevermore.

My God, my God, why hast thou forsaken me? why art thou so far from helping me, and from the words of my roaring?
O my God, I cry in the daytime, but thou hearest not; and in the night season, and am not silent.
But thou art holy, O thou that inhabitest the praises of Israel.
Our fathers trusted in thee: they trusted, and thou didst deliver them.
They cried unto thee, and were delivered: they trusted in thee, and were not confounded.
But I am a worm, and no man; a reproach of men, and despised of the people.
All they that see me laugh me to scorn: they shoot out the lip, they shake the head, saying,
He trusted on the Lord that he would deliver him: let him deliver him, seeing he delighted in him.
But thou art he that took me out of the womb: thou didst make me hope when I was upon my mother's breasts.
I was cast upon thee from the womb: thou art my God from my mother's belly.
Be not far from me; for trouble is near; for there is none to help.
Many bulls have compassed me: strong bulls of Bashan have beset me round.
They gaped upon me with their mouths, as a ravening and a roaring lion.

I am poured out like water, and all my bones are out of joint: my heart is like wax; it is melted in the midst of my bowels.

My strength is dried up like a potsherd; and my tongue cleaveth to my jaws; and thou hast brought me into the dust of death.

For dogs have compassed me: the assembly of the wicked have enclosed me: they pierced my hands and my feet.

I may tell all my bones: they look and stare upon me.

They part my garments among them, and cast lots upon my vesture.

But be not thou far from me, O Lord: O my strength, haste thee to help me.

Deliver my soul from the sword; my darling from the power of the dog.

Save me from the lion's mouth: for thou hast heard me from the horns of the unicorns.

I will declare thy name unto my brethren: in the midst of the congregation will I praise thee.

Ye that fear the Lord, praise him; all ye the seed of Jacob, glorify him; and fear him, all ye the seed of Israel.

For he hath not despised nor abhorred the affliction of the afflicted; neither hath he hid his face from him; but when he cried unto him, he heard.

My praise shall be of thee in the great congregation: I will pay my vows before them that fear him.

The meek shall eat and be satisfied: they shall praise the Lord that seek him: your heart shall live forever.

All the ends of the world shall remember and turn unto the Lord: and all the kindreds of the nations shall worship before thee.

For the kingdom is the Lord's: and he is the governor

among the nations.

All they that be fat upon earth shall eat and worship: all they that go down to the dust shall bow before him: and none can keep alive his own soul.

A seed shall serve him; it shall be accounted to the Lord for a generation.

They shall come, and shall declare his righteousness unto a people that shall be born, that he hath done this.

PSALM 22

In thee, O Lord, do I put my trust; let me never be ashamed: deliver me in thy righteousness. Bow down thine ear to me; deliver me speedily: be thou my strong rock, for a house of defense to save me.

For thou art my rock and my fortress; therefore for thy name's sake lead me, and guide me.

Pull me out of the net that they have laid privily for me: for thou art my strength.

Into thine hand I commit my spirit: thou hast redeemed me, O Lord God of truth.

I have hated them that regard lying vanities: but I trust in the Lord.

I will be glad and rejoice in thy mercy: for thou hast considered my trouble; thou hast known my soul in adversities;

And hast not shut me up into the hand of the enemy: thou hast set my feet in a large room.

Have mercy upon me, O Lord, for I am in trouble: mine eye is consumed with grief, yea, my soul and my belly.

For my life is spent with grief, and my years with sighing: my strength faileth because of mine iniquity, and my bones are consumed.

I was a reproach among all mine enemies, but especially among my neighbours, and a fear to mine acquaintance: they that did see me without fled from me.

I am forgotten as a dead man out of mind: I am like a broken vessel.

For I have heard the slander of many: fear was on every side: while they took counsel together against me, they devised to take away my life.

But I trusted in thee, O Lord: I said, Thou art my God.

My times are in thy hand: deliver me from the hand of mine enemies, and from them that persecute me.

Make thy face to shine upon thy servant: save me for thy mercies' sake.

Let me not be ashamed, O Lord; for I have called upon thee: let the wicked be ashamed, and let them be silent in the grave.

Let the lying lips be put to silence; which speak grievous things proudly and contemptuously against the righteous.

Oh how great is thy goodness, which thou hast laid up for them that fear thee; which thou hast wrought for them that trust in thee before the sons of men!

Thou shalt hide them in the secret of thy presence from the pride of man: thou shalt keep them secretly in a pavilion from the strife of tongues.

Blessed be the Lord: for he hath showed me his marvellous kindness in a strong city.

For I said in my haste, I am cut off from before thine eyes: nevertheless thou heardest the voice of my supplications when I cried unto thee.

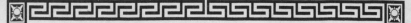

O love the Lord, all ye his saints: for the Lord preserveth the faithful, and plentifully rewardeth the proud doer of good courage, and he shall strengthen your heart, all ye that hope in the Lord.

PSALM 31

Behold, the eye of the Lord is upon them that fear him, upon them that hope in his mercy; To deliver their soul from death, and to keep them alive in famine.
Our soul waiteth for the Lord: he is our help and our shield.
For our heart shall rejoice in him, because we have trusted in his holy name.
Let thy mercy, O Lord, be upon us, according as we hope in thee.

PSALM 33:18-22

O Lord, rebuke me not in thy wrath: neither chasten me in thy hot displeasure.
For thine arrows stick fast in me, and thy hand presseth me sore.
There is no soundness in my flesh because of thine anger; neither is there any rest in my bones because of my sin.
For mine iniquities are gone over mine head: as a heavy burden they are too heavy for me.

My wounds stink and are corrupt because of my foolishness.

I am troubled; I am bowed down greatly; I go mourning all the day long.

For my loins are filled with a loathsome disease: and there is no soundness in my flesh.

I am feeble and sore broken: I have roared by reason of the disquietness of my heart.

Lord, all my desire is before thee; and my groaning is not hid from thee.

My heart panteth, my strength faileth me: as for the light of mine eyes, it also is gone from me.

My lovers and my friends stand aloof from my sore; and my kinsmen stand afar off.

They also that seek after my life lay snares for me: and they that seek my hurt speak mischievous things, and imagine deceits all the day long.

But I, as a deaf man, heard not; and I was as a dumb man that openeth not his mouth.

Thus I was as a man that heareth not, and in whose mouth are no reproofs.

For in thee, O Lord, do I hope: thou wilt hear, O Lord my God.

For I said, Hear me, lest otherwise they should rejoice over me: when my foot slippeth, they magnify themselves against me.

For I am ready to halt, and my sorrow is continually before me.

For I will declare mine iniquity; I will be sorry for my sin.

But mine enemies are lively, and they are strong: and they that hate me wrongfully are multiplied.

They also that render evil for good are mine adver-

saries; because I follow the thing that good is.
Forsake me not, O Lord: O my God, be not far from me.
Make haste to help me, O Lord my salvation.

PSALM 38

Behold, thou hast made my days as a hand-
breadth; and mine age is as nothing before
thee: verily every man at his best state is altogether vanity. Selah.
Surely every man walketh in a vain show: surely they
are disquieted in vain: he heapeth up riches, and
knoweth not who shall gather them.
And now, Lord, what wait I for? my hope is in thee.

PSALM 39:5-7

As the hart panteth after the water brooks, so
panteth my soul after thee, O God.
My soul thirsteth for God, for the living God:
when shall I come and appear before God?
My tears have been my food day and night, while
they continually say unto me, Where is thy God?
When I remember these things, I pour out my soul in
me: for I had gone with the multitude, I went with
them to the house of God, with the voice of joy
and praise, with a multitude that kept holyday.
Why art thou cast down, O my soul? and why art thou
disquieted in me? hope thou in God: for I shall yet
praise him for the help of his countenance.

O my God, my soul is cast down within me: therefore
will I remember thee from the land of Jordan, and
of the Hermonites, from the hill Mizar.
Deep calleth unto deep at the noise of thy water-
spouts: all thy waves and thy billows are gone
over me.
Yet the Lord will command his loving-kindness in the
daytime, and in the night his song shall be with
me, and my prayer unto the God of my life.
I will say unto God my rock, Why hast thou forgotten
me? why go I mourning because of the oppression
of the enemy?
As with a sword in my bones, mine enemies reproach
me; while they say daily unto me, Where is thy
God?
Why art thou cast down, O my soul? and why art thou
disquieted within me? hope thou in God: for I
shall yet praise him, who is the health of my
countenance, and my God.

PSALM 42

Judge me, O God, and plead my cause against
an ungodly nation: O deliver me from the
deceitful and unjust man.
For thou art the God of my strength: why dost
thou cast me off? why go I mourning because of
the oppression of the enemy?
O send out thy light and thy truth: let them lead me;
let them bring me unto thy holy hill, and to thy
tabernacles.
Then will I go unto the altar of God, unto God my

exceeding joy: yea, upon the harp will I praise
thee, O God my God.

Why art thou cast down, O my soul? and why art thou
disquieted within me? hope in God: for I shall yet
praise him, who is the health of my countenance,
and my God.

PSALM 43

I n thee, O Lord, do I put my trust: let me never
be put to confusion.
Deliver me in thy righteousness, and cause
me to escape: incline thine ear unto me, and save
me.

Be thou my strong habitation, whereunto I may continually resort: thou hast given commandment to
save me; for thou art my rock and my fortress.

Deliver me, O my God, out of the hand of the wicked,
out of the hand of the unrighteous and cruel man.

For thou art my hope, O Lord God: thou art my trust
from my youth.

By thee have I been holden up from the womb: thou
art he that took me out of my mother's bowels: my
praise shall be continually of thee.

I am as a wonder unto many; but thou art my strong
refuge.

Let my mouth be filled with thy praise and with thy
honour all the day.

Cast me not off in the time of old age; forsake me not
when my strength faileth.

For mine enemies speak against me; and they that lay
wait for my soul take counsel together,

Saying, God hath forsaken him: persecute and take
him; for there is none to deliver him.

O God, be not far from me: O my God, make haste for
my help.
Let them be confounded and consumed that are
adversaries to my soul; let them be covered with
reproach and dishonour that seek my hurt.
But I will hope continually, and will yet praise thee
more and more.
My mouth shall show forth thy righteousness and thy
salvation all the day; for I know not the numbers
thereof.
I will go in the strength of the Lord God: I will make
mention of thy righteousness, even of thine only.
O God, thou hast taught me from my youth: and hith-
erto have I declared thy wondrous works.
Now also when I am old and greyheaded, O God, forsake me not; until I have showed thy strength
unto this generation, and thy power to every one
that is to come.
Thy righteousness also, O God, is very high, who hast
done great things: O God, who is like unto thee!
Thou, which hast showed me great and sore troubles,
shalt quicken me again, and shalt bring me up
again from the depths of the earth.
Thou shalt increase my greatness, and comfort me on
every side.
I will also praise thee with the psaltery, even thy truth,
O my God: unto thee will I sing with the harp, O
thou Holy One of Israel.
My lips shall greatly rejoice when I sing unto thee;
and my soul, which thou hast redeemed.
My tongue also shall talk of thy righteousness all the
day long: for they are confounded, for they are
brought unto shame, that seek my hurt.

PSALM 71

Thou art my hiding place and my shield: I hope in thy word.

Depart from me, ye evildoers: for I will keep the commandments of my God.

Uphold me according unto thy word, that I may live: and let me not be ashamed of my hope.

PSALM 119:114-116

I wait for the Lord, my soul doth wait, and in his word do I hope.

My soul waiteth for the Lord more than they that watch for the morning: I say, more than they that watch for the morning.

Let Israel hope in the Lord: for with the Lord there is mercy, and with him is plenteous redemption.

PSALM 130:5-7

Praise ye the Lord. Praise the Lord, O my soul. While I live will I praise the Lord: I will sing praises unto my God while I have any being.

Put not your trust in princes, nor in the son of man, in whom there is no help.

His breath goeth forth, he returneth to his earth; in that very day his thoughts perish.

Happy is he that hath the God of Jacob for his help, whose hope is in the Lord his God:

Which made heaven, and earth, the sea, and all that therein is: which keepeth truth forever:

Which executeth judgment for the oppressed: which

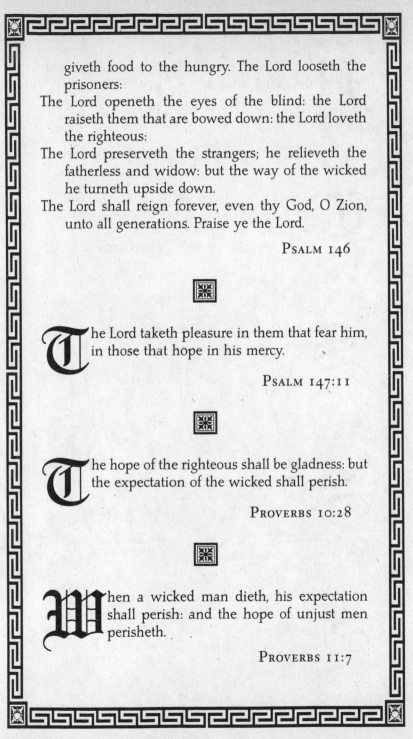

giveth food to the hungry. The Lord looseth the prisoners:

The Lord openeth the eyes of the blind: the Lord raiseth them that are bowed down: the Lord loveth the righteous:

The Lord preserveth the strangers; he relieveth the fatherless and widow: but the way of the wicked he turneth upside down.

The Lord shall reign forever, even thy God, O Zion, unto all generations. Praise ye the Lord.

PSALM 146

The Lord taketh pleasure in them that fear him, in those that hope in his mercy.

PSALM 147:11

The hope of the righteous shall be gladness: but the expectation of the wicked shall perish.

PROVERBS 10:28

When a wicked man dieth, his expectation shall perish: and the hope of unjust men perisheth.

PROVERBS 11:7

Hope deferred maketh the heart sick: but when the desire cometh, it is a tree of life.

PROVERBS 13:12

The wicked is driven away in his wickedness: but the righteous hath hope in his death.

PROVERBS 14:32

Seest thou a man wise in his own conceit? there is more hope of a fool than of him.

PROVERBS 26:12

Seest thou a man that is hasty in his words? there is more hope of a fool than of him.

PROVERBS 29:20

For to him that is joined to all the living there is hope: for a living dog is better than a dead lion.

ECCLESIASTES 9:4

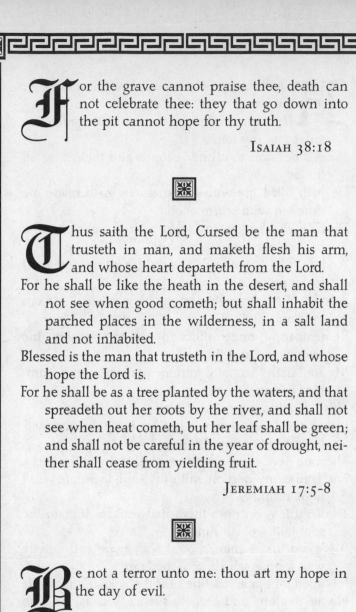

For the grave cannot praise thee, death cannot celebrate thee: they that go down into the pit cannot hope for thy truth.

ISAIAH 38:18

Thus saith the Lord, Cursed be the man that trusteth in man, and maketh flesh his arm, and whose heart departeth from the Lord.

For he shall be like the heath in the desert, and shall not see when good cometh; but shall inhabit the parched places in the wilderness, in a salt land and not inhabited.

Blessed is the man that trusteth in the Lord, and whose hope the Lord is.

For he shall be as a tree planted by the waters, and that spreadeth out her roots by the river, and shall not see when heat cometh, but her leaf shall be green; and shall not be careful in the year of drought, neither shall cease from yielding fruit.

JEREMIAH 17:5-8

Be not a terror unto me: thou art my hope in the day of evil.

JEREMIAH 17:17

He hath bent his bow, and set me as a mark for the arrow.

He hath caused the arrows of his quiver to enter into my reins.

I was a derision to all my people; and their song all the day.

He hath filled me with bitterness, he hath made me drunken with wormwood.

He hath also broken my teeth with gravel stones, he hath covered me with ashes.

And thou hast removed my soul far off from peace: I forgat prosperity.

And I said, My strength and my hope is perished from the Lord:

Remembering mine affliction and my misery, the wormwood and the gall.

My soul hath them still in remembrance, and is humbled in me.

This I recall to my mind, therefore have I hope.

It is of the Lord's mercies that we are not consumed, because his compassions fail not.

They are new every morning: great is thy faithfulness.

The Lord is my portion, saith my soul; therefore will I hope in him.

The Lord is good unto them that wait for him, to the soul that seeketh him.

It is good that a man should both hope and quietly wait for the salvation of the Lord.

It is good for a man that he bear the yoke in his youth.

He sitteth alone and keepeth silence, because he hath borne it upon him.

He putteth his mouth in the dust; if so be there may be hope.

He giveth his cheek to him that smiteth him: he is filled full with reproach.

For the Lord will not cast off forever:
But though he cause grief, yet will he have compassion according to the multitude of his mercies.

LAMENTATIONS 3:12-32

And I will give her her vineyards from thence, and the valley of Achor for a door of hope: and she shall sing there, as in the days of her youth, and as in the day when she came up out of the land of Egypt.

HOSEA 2:15

The Lord also shall roar out of Zion, and utter his voice from Jerusalem; and the heavens and the earth shall shake: but the Lord will be the hope of his people, and the strength of the children of Israel.

JOEL 3:16

For David speaketh concerning him, I foresaw the Lord always before my face, for he is on my right hand, that I should not be moved: Therefore did my heart rejoice, and my tongue was glad; moreover also my flesh shall rest in hope:

Because thou wilt not leave my soul in hell, neither
wilt thou suffer thine Holy One to see corruption.

ACTS 2:25-27

nd have hope toward God, which they
themselves also allow, that there shall be a
resurrection of the dead, both of the just and
unjust.

ACTS 24:15

herefore being justified by faith, we have
peace with God through our Lord Jesus
Christ:
By whom also we have access by faith into this grace
wherein we stand, and rejoice in hope of the glory
of God.
And not only so, but we glory in tribulations also:
knowing that tribulation worketh patience;
And patience, experience; and experience, hope:
And hope maketh not ashamed; because the love of
God is shed abroad in our hearts by the Holy
Ghost which is given unto us.

ROMANS 5:1-5

For we know that the whole creation groaneth and travaileth in pain together until now.

And not only they, but ourselves also, which have the first fruits of the Spirit, even we ourselves groan within ourselves, waiting for the adoption, to wit, the redemption of our body.

For we are saved by hope: but hope that is seen is not hope: for what a man seeth, why doth he yet hope for?

But if we hope for that we see not, then do we with patience wait for it.

ROMANS 8:22-25

We then that are strong ought to bear the infirmities of the weak, and not to please ourselves.

Let every one of us please his neighbour for his good to edification.

For even Christ pleased not himself; but, as it is written, The reproaches of them that reproached thee fell on me.

For whatsoever things were written aforetime were written for our learning, that we through patience and comfort of the scriptures might have hope.

ROMANS 15:1-4

ow the God of hope fill you with all joy and peace in believing, that ye may abound in hope, through the power of the Holy Ghost.

ROMANS 15:13

r saith he it altogether for our sakes? For our sakes, no doubt, this is written: that he that ploweth should plow in hope; and that he that thresheth in hope should be partaker of his hope.

1 CORINTHIANS 9:10

or if the dead rise not, then is not Christ raised:
And if Christ be not raised, your faith is vain ye are yet in your sins.
Then they also which are fallen asleep in Christ are perished.
If in this life only we have hope in Christ, we are of all men most miserable.
But now is Christ risen from the dead, and become the first fruits of them that slept.
For since by man came death, by man came also the resurrection of the dead.
For as in Adam all die, even so in Christ shall all be made alive.

1 CORINTHIANS 15:16-22

For as the sufferings of Christ abound in us, so our consolation also aboundeth by Christ. And whether we be afflicted, it is for your consolation and salvation, which is effectual in the enduring of the same sufferings which we also suffer: or whether we be comforted, it is for your consolation and salvation.

And our hope of you is steadfast, knowing, that as ye are partakers of the sufferings, so shall ye be also of the consolation.

2 CORINTHIANS 1:5-7

According to my earnest expectation and my hope, that in nothing I shall be ashamed, but that with all boldness, as always, so now also Christ shall be magnified in my body, whether it be by life, or by death.

PHILIPPIANS 1:20

We give thanks to God and the Father of our Lord Jesus Christ, praying always for you, Since we heard of your faith in Christ Jesus, and of the love which ye have to all the saints,

For the hope which is laid up for you in heaven, whereof ye heard before in the word of the truth of the gospel;

Which is come unto you, as it is in all the world; and bringeth forth fruit, as it doth also in you, since the day ye heard of it, and knew the grace of God in truth:

As ye also learned of Epaphras our dear fellow servant, who is for you a faithful minister of Christ;

Who also declared unto us your love in the Spirit.

COLOSSIANS 1:3-8

If ye continue in the faith grounded and settled, and be not moved away from the hope of the gospel, which ye have heard, and which was preached to every creature which is under heaven; whereof I, Paul, am made a minister;

Who now rejoice in my sufferings for you, and fill up that which is behind of the afflictions of Christ in my flesh for his body's sake, which is the church:

Whereof I am made a minister, according to the dispensation of God which is given to me for you, to fulfill the word of God;

Even the mystery which hath been hid from ages and from generations, but now is made manifest to his saints:

To whom God would make known what is the riches of the glory of this mystery among the Gentiles; which is Christ in you, the hope of glory:

Whom we preach, warning every man, and teaching every man in all wisdom; that we may present every man perfect in Christ Jesus:

Whereunto I also labour, striving according to his working, which worketh in me mightily.

COLOSSIANS 1:23-29

or if we believe that Jesus died and rose again, even so them also which sleep in Jesus will God bring with him.

For this we say unto you by the word of the Lord, that we which are alive and remain unto the coming of the Lord shall not prevent them which are asleep.

For the Lord himself shall descend from heaven with a shout, with the voice of the archangel, and with the trump of God: and the dead in Christ shall rise first:

Then we which are alive and remain shall be caught up together with them in the clouds, to meet the Lord in the air: and so shall we ever be with the Lord.

1 THESSALONIANS 4:14-17

ow our Lord Jesus Christ himself, and God, even our Father, which hath loved us, and hath given us everlasting consolation and good hope through grace,

Comfort your hearts, and stablish you in every good word and work.

2 THESSALONIANS 2:16-17

For the grace of God that bringeth salvation hath appeared to all men,
Teaching us that, denying ungodliness and worldly lusts, we should live soberly, righteously, and godly, in this present world;
Looking for that blessed hope, and the glorious appearing of the great God and our Saviour Jesus Christ;
Who gave himself for us, that he might redeem us from all iniquity, and purify unto himself a peculiar people, zealous of good works.

TITUS 2:11-14

But after that the kindness and love of God our Saviour toward man appeared,
Not by works of righteousness which we have done, but according to his mercy he saved us, by the washing of regeneration, and renewing of the Holy Ghost;
Which he shed on us abundantly through Jesus Christ our Saviour;
That being justified by his grace, we should be made heirs according to the hope of eternal life.

TITUS 3:4-7

For every house is builded by some man; but he that built all things is God.
And Moses verily was faithful in all his house, as a servant, for a testimony of those things which were to be spoken after;

But Christ as a son over his own house; whose house are we, if we hold fast the confidence and the rejoicing of the hope firm unto the end.

HEBREWS 3:4-6

For the law made nothing perfect, but the bringing in of a better hope did; by the which we draw nigh unto God.

HEBREWS 7:19

Blessed be the God and Father of our Lord Jesus Christ, which according to his abundant mercy hath begotten us again unto a lively hope by the resurrection of Jesus Christ from the dead,
To an inheritance incorruptible, and undefiled, and that fadeth not away, reserved in heaven for you,
Who are kept by the power of God through faith unto salvation ready to be revealed in the last time.

1 PETER 1:3-5

Who by him do believe in God, that raised him up from the dead, and gave him glory; that your faith and hope might be in God.
Seeing ye have purified your souls in obeying the truth through the Spirit unto unfeigned love of the

brethren, see that ye love one another with a pure heart fervently:

Being born again, not of corruptible seed, but of incorruptible, by the word of God, which liveth and abideth forever.

For all flesh is as grass, and all the glory of man as the flower of grass. The grass withereth, and the flower thereof falleth away:

But the word of the Lord endureth forever. And this is the word which by the gospel is preached unto you.

I Peter 1:21-25

And who is he that will harm you, if ye be followers of that which is good?

But and if ye suffer for righteousness' sake, happy are ye: and be not afraid of their terror, neither be troubled;

But sanctify the Lord God in your hearts: and be ready always to give an answer to every man that asketh you a reason of the hope that is in you with meekness and fear:

Having a good conscience; that, whereas they speak evil of you, as of evildoers, they may be ashamed that falsely accuse your good conversation in Christ.

For it is better, if the will of God be so, that ye suffer for well doing, than for evil doing.

I Peter 3:13-17

And every man that hath this hope in him purifieth himself, even as he is pure.

1 JOHN 3:3